The Practical Dreamer

the Do's and Don'ts of Mastering a Small Business

Ken Boyar

The Practical Dreamer
Do's and Don'ts of Mastering a Small Business

iUniverse books may be ordered through booksellers or by contacting:
iUniverse
1663 Liberty Drive
Bloomington, IN 47403
www.iuniverse.com
1-800-Authors (1-800-288-4677)

Because of the dynamic nature of the Internet, any Web addresses or links contained in this book may have changed since publication and may no longer be valid. The views expressed in this work are solely those of the author and do not necessarily reflect the views of the publisher, and the publisher hereby disclaims any responsibility for them.

ISBN: 978-1-4502-2733-9 (pbk)
ISBN: 978-1-4502-2735-3 (ebk)
ISBN: 978-1-4502-2734-6 (hbk)

Printed in the United States of America
iUniverse rev. date: 6/14/10

Table of Contents

I INTRODUCTION

For nearly thirty years, I have been in the accounting and finance profession. Most accountants start their careers auditing the books and records of small businesses, and I was no exception. I found a greater challenge, however, when I moved on to become a controller within one company and then worked over the years in a variety of businesses and industries.

In many small businesses, a controller is asked to wear several hats. I was not sure at first whether I would like this new challenge. After all, I was trained as an accountant, and that is what I knew. Now I was no longer reporting only historical information to the owners, i.e., the results of the transactions from the month prior. I was being asked to comment on where the business could improve in the future. A whole new world of thinking opened up. No longer was I seen as purely a cost to the company. Now I was an asset who could contribute to the bottom line in a way that I had not been able to before.

In 2000, I made the next great leap and started a business of my own, offering controller-level services to small businesses on a part-time basis. Today I have several employees and a thriving business. These last ten years have been phenomenal. When I look back at my experiences prior to owning my business, I see that while they laid a good foundation for my current work, in many ways they only scratched the surface.

Most controllers work full-time for a single company. For ten years now this business of mine has afforded me something far greater: to be of service to more than fifty businesses, including a solid mix of service and product companies — both start-ups and established businesses. My strength has always been in talking numbers but my experiences now led me to serve my clients in ways I had never imagined. I could point out where there were gaps in their operations, where their business plans may have gone astray, where new sales and marketing approaches were necessary, and much more.

I had graduated to the role of business manager.

People choose to start a business for many reasons. Most have good reasons and yet some can make poor choices. Start a business because it's what you've always wanted to do. Start a business because there is a particular industry that you've always dreamed of being part of. Start a business to be excellent at what you do. I want you to be all of these things but, most important, I want you to be prepared. Read this book and take with you whatever seems appropriate for your situation. Use it as a reference that you can come back to periodically to remind yourself of the important do's and don'ts of good business practice.

I have had clients who made smart decisions and prospered. You will hear about some of them. Others made poor decisions and suffered as a result. I've seen them both first-hand. I don't write about the isolated cases but about the regular occurrences — although one might say that some of them are quite "irregular." Good decision-making is not a guarantee of success but it certainly puts the odds in your favor.

As for the "do's and don'ts": some of them are quite simple and yet have eluded so many entrepreneurs. While I cannot possibly cover all situations and issues, I will say, that if you follow the basic rules of this book you will gain a clear understanding of what you're up against and learn how to overcome the obstacles. Once you have mastered the basic principles, new challenges will be easier to face. Knowledge will serve you well. It always does.

Many of you may be thinking of someone you know who has defied the odds; someone who has not followed these basic principles yet has become quite successful. And for everyone you know, I would bet that I know five more. It's not impossible to abandon the basic principles and succeed. What I'm referring to is about playing the odds. For every five people I know who have defied the odds, I know one hundred who stuck to these sound business practices and were successful. So I ask you: how would you like to operate? On the side of risk or with the majority? I know people who find risk exciting. When it comes to business, these risk-takers often lead hard lives. When the risks pay off, all is good and everyone goes home happy. When the risks turn bad, as they often do, they find themselves swimming upstream.

We can't all make the right choices in business. You can be, however, as informed as possible. With the necessary information, you can proceed to be as good a business owner as possible. Your venture may be a dream you have always had, and I for one want to see it come alive and flourish. My goal is to help you get there.

Let's begin the journey.

II THE FIRST STEP TO PRACTICAL DREAMING

L et's talk about this dream of yours. How often have you heard someone say that you need to develop a good business plan before opening the doors? I've heard it countless times and advise my clients entering into new business ventures to do the same. But over the years I've come across more and more people who failed to create a formal written plan and now they are suffering the consequences.

Why would so many people skip over something so essential? Only recently have I come up with the answer — an explanation so powerful that even the best lesson in business and accounting cannot overcome it.

A BUSINESS PLAN TELLS US WHAT IT WILL TAKE TO PROSPER. SOMETIMES, HOWEVER, WE DON'T WANT TO KNOW THE BAD NEWS UP FRONT. THAT KNOWLEDGE MAY LITERALLY KILL THE DREAM.

Whether you dream of owning your own business, of owning a business in a particular industry, or of becoming an entrepreneur and all that entails, who wants to see their dream shot down? Add a bit of psychology and we could probably say that those who don't write a formal business plan know in their hearts that their venture probably is not going to work. I don't know of any studies on this phenomenon but my gut feeling is that there are many who fit this category.

If you came to me and said, "You know, Ken, I have always wanted to open a restaurant. I have deep pockets and while the outlook doesn't look great, it's something that I must do. If it doesn't work, so be it. I will move on."

I would only offer the following before getting down to evaluating the numbers: "Go for it. Who am I to interfere with your dream?"

MEET BETSY...ENTREPRENEUR AND SUCCESSFUL BUSINESSPERSON

I have a wonderful client, Betsy, who is in the business of selling art. Before she ever opened her doors, she came to me in order to get a good business plan on paper. Like most people, she did not have deep pockets. Betsy had a lot to lose and was about to invest her entire life savings.

"Betsy," I said, "take a deep breath and tell yourself that your life savings is extremely precious to you and that under no circumstances will you jeopardize it. We're going to do things right from the start and the start is RIGHT NOW.

Betsy, remember how I told you that many people don't make a formal business plan because they fear they'll destroy their dream. Well, here is where they went wrong, so listen up. In many cases, you don't need to abandon the dream but only to re-think the plan. In fact, the plan may need to go through several changes before it is complete and sound.

So do you see what happened to those people who either didn't write a plan at all or simply abandoned their plan after the first try? *Most likely, they only needed to go through several revisions until it looked like a workable plan!*

Got it?"

She had.

"Now let's move on so that I can tell you what this plan should include. First off, do you recall, Betsy, that I've been using the words formal business plan? In a nutshell, it simply means that you're actually going to write it down."

I told her about a potential client who claimed that he had a plan all laid out in his head and that it was probably good enough. Sorry. It's not. When our words and thoughts hit the paper (or the computer screen), we discover that many elements in that plan may need revision.

Along the way, I directed Betsy to some of my favorite readings on how to develop a good business plans. I always suggest that my clients read one or more of them before setting out on the task of writing their own. There is Jim Horan's book, *The One Page Business Plan* (1997), *The E-Myth* by Michael Gerber (1995), and many others. Software programs are also out there, which offer the same advice although I do favor the texts. Nonetheless, I instructed Betsy on what I call the "bones" or the "must-haves" in every plan.

I started her out with a broad guideline. Every plan has two overall parts: the text and the financials, and they should be tackled in that order. The text outlines in your own words what the business is all about and includes a detailed description of the product or service, how you believe you can accomplish your goals, the marketing plan you will use, knowledge about your competition, and so on. You will learn a great deal here.

Oh yes, another piece of advice that I offered Betsy. "Wouldn't you agree that it's a good idea to let someone else read your plan for a dose of that old constructive criticism?"

Betsy put up her hand as if signaling me to stop. "Makes all the sense in the world to have someone read my plan," she said, "but you don't know my friends. Some of them can be quite pessimistic, so I'm going to have to choose my audience well."

While you want someone trustworthy to read it, don't be shy, I told her, about giving the text to someone whom she regards as too pessimistic. We all have them in our lives, I assured her. Take a deep breath and let them have their say. Draw what is meaningful from their remarks. You just might find a golden nugget. And when you've listened and made the changes that you deem appropriate, give yourself a pat on the back for a job well done. But don't rest the pen. It's now on to the financials.

If you wanted to see the whites of someone's eyes, it would be Betsy's at this moment. You know the look — where your brain goes into hibernation over the mere thought of numbers. I reassured her. Yes, it's wonderful if you're financially savvy. Certainly, not all of us can make that claim. "Betsy, there are no worries. You only need to understand the basics. I will do all the financial calculating. You just need to supply the ideas."

Many accountants create business plans as a regular part of their work. You may even have some friends in the financial world that can do the same. By all means, if you need to pay for the service, do so. The money spent up front is some of the wisest money you'll spend in your whole business life.

I explained to her exactly what this exercise would accomplish. The numbers must ultimately be a reflection of the text you have already written. They are usually laid out in a "cash-flow" format, which takes all the income and expenses and places each one in a monthly column in which the specific revenue or expense will actually occur. This is normally projected out for at least two years (*See example below*).

EYZ Tool Distribution Company
Cash Projection for the year 2010
Initial Year of Operations

	Jan	Feb	March	April
Opening Cash Balance	$0	$18,979	$13,807	$7,386
Incoming Cash projected:				
Cash receipts from customers (1)		$10,000	$10,000	$10,000
Capital Infusion of owner(s)	$30,000			
Third party cash infusion				$5,000
Total Incoming Cash	$30,000	$10,000	$10,000	$15,000
Outgoing Cash projected:				
Offset set-up costs	$1,000	$500		
Security deposits	$7,000			
Payroll	$4,200	$4,200	$4,200	$4,200
Payroll taxes	$321	$321	$321	$321
Health benefits (50% contributory)	$900	$900	$900	$900
Commission to salespeople (paid quarterly)				$2,000
Rent (includes utilities)	$3,500	$3,500	$3,500	$3,500
Accounting services (retainers)	$0	$500	$500	$500
Legal services (non-retainer, start-up cost)			$2,000	
Travel	$0	$2,500	$2,000	$2,000
Meals & customer entertainment	$0	$1,250	$1,000	$1,000
Marketing services (retainer)	$500	$500	$500	$500
Purchase of new equipment (on credit)		$1,000	$1,000	$1,000
Property insurance (paid annually)	$1,200			
Workers comp insurance (paid per payroll)	$150	$150	$150	$150
Unemployment insurance (paid quarterly)				$680
Telephone and other communications	$250	$250	$250	$250
Office supplies and other expenses	$0	$100	$100	$100
Total Outgoing Cash	$11,021	$15,171	$16,421	$17,101
Net Monthly Cash	$18,979	($5,171)	($6,421)	($2,101)
Ending Cash Balance	$18,979	$13,807	$7,386	$5,285

(1) should be itemized customer by customer

As this example shows, the owner has wisely capitalized the business with $30,000. Even though the months of June and July show a rather low ending balance, the owner can see that without realizing a $5,000 cash investment from an outside third party, those same months would end with a deficit balance. Note, however, that the cash position will recover nicely in subsequent months as long as the business meets its sales projections.

May	June	2010 July	Aug	Sept	Oct	Nov	Dec	TOTAL
$5,285	$6,164	$5,042	$2,481	$10,260	$17,138	$18,217	$24,796	$0
$15,000	$15,000	$15,000	$20,000	$20,000	$20,000	$20,000	$20,000	$175,000
								$30,000
								$5,000
$15,000	$15,000	$15,000	$20,000	$20,000	$20,000	$20,000	$20,000	$210,000
								$1,500
								$7,000
$4,200	$4,200	$4,200	$4,200	$4,200	$4,200	$4,200	$4,200	$50,400
$321	$321	$321	$321	$321	$321	$321	$321	$3,856
$900	$900	$900	$900	$900		$900	$900	$10,800
		$4,000			$5,500			$11,500
$3,500	$3,500	$3,500	$3,500	$3,500	$3,500	$3,500	$3,500	$42,000
$500	$500	$500	$500	$500	$500	$500	$500	$5,500
		$2,000						$4,000
$1,800	$1,800	$1,200	$1,200	$1,800	$2,000	$2,000	$1,200	$19,500
$900	$900	$600	$600	$900	$1,000	$1,000	$600	$9,750
$500	$500	$500	$500	$500	$500	$500	$500	$6,000
$1,000	$1,000	$1,000						$6,000
								$1,200
$150	$150	$150	$150	$150	$150	$150	$150	$1,800
		$340			$0			$1,020
$250	$250	$250	$250	$250	$250	$250	$250	$3,000
$100	$100	$100	$100	$100	$100	$100	$100	$1,100
$14,121	$16,121	$17,561	$12,221	$13,121	$18,921	$13,421	$12,221	$177,426
$879	($1,121)	($2,561)	$7,779	$6,879	$1,079	$6,579	$7,779	$32,574
$6,164	$5,042	$2,481	$10,260	$17,138	$18,217	$24,796	$32,574	$32,574

This time, she leaned forward as if she were about to put her hands around my throat. "Two years! I'm guessing at some of the numbers for this year. How am I supposed to be accurate about next year's numbers?"

She was absolutely correct. It is quite difficult. A good accountant will ask you the kind of pertinent questions that should make this task easier but remember — these are your (and the accountant's) best guesses. But here's the thing. Even though they are guesses, they are *educated* guesses that are essential in forming the plan as a whole.

Let me ask a question as a way of giving you an example. Isn't it better to assume that the cost of health insurance will rise by 15 percent in the second year (which is the industry average) than to be caught off guard by not including any estimate at all? It's just that simple. An educated guess is better than no guess at all.

Most importantly, I told her, once all the numbers are in place, she would have answers to the following and many other questions:

1. Will I need more or less money to start the company than initially planned?

2. If I am going to run out of money, in what month can I expect that to happen?

3. If I need to secure a loan, in what month should I apply for that loan in order to have the cash when I need it?

4. What amount of income or sales do I need to generate every month in order to cover my basic expenses?

I told her not to be discouraged by the fact that the plan would need to go through several stages before we can call it complete. Her plan did indeed need several revisions but Betsy was amazed by the results. It required some hard thinking in many areas but she did it. No, she didn't open her art gallery when she planned. In fact, she delayed four months before opening the doors, but she opened those doors with a good sound plan in hand. Betsy lived up to the numbers in her plan after her first year but there were more lessons to be learned. Future chapters will get into some of the very things that I told Betsy at the start.

ONE STEP AT A TIME

So, all you entrepreneurs — now that I have told you not to stop dreaming big, let's take one step back for a moment. If you're an experienced businessperson, then you already know that you need to position your products and/or services correctly. Sometimes, that means trying to figure out how to run a financially successful business as a local one — not as the mega-giant of the industry you had perhaps anticipated. Yes, your long-term plan may include mega-giant dreams, but when you are in the start-up phase, short-term, two-year plans take precedent over long term.

One of my favorite stories is that of the pizza shop owner who must have had a very savvy marketing background or perhaps knew some of the same savvy marketers that I know. The story goes like this:

One day, John was walking down the street and realized that he would like to have pizza for lunch. In front of him he saw a sign in a window that read:

"Best pizza in the world," but when he looked inside the pizzeria he saw no customers. He walked on a few steps and came to a second pizza shop. Its sign read: "Best pizza in town." He saw only a few customers inside and again decided to walk on. Before reaching the corner, he noticed yet another pizza shop. This one had a line of customers out the door and not one available seat inside. He noticed the sign in the window: "Best pizza on the block."

And so goes the tale. The owner of "best pizza on the block" was a practical dreamer. And as such, his strategy paid off in spades. He knew not to bite off more than he could chew. He had a business plan that called for a proper positioning within his market. Perhaps he began his entrepreneurial life thinking he was going to have the biggest and most successful pizza shop that this country has ever known. Along the way, with good guidance, he realized that there was a better short-term plan.

Don't get me wrong. We all know of some huge pizza franchises with locations all around the country. Yes, dream big if the concept of being a franchise-maker interests you. But I can assure you that the short-term, two-year plan for a new business should resemble that of our local pizza shop owner who knew, before anything else, that he needed to serve the best pizza on the block.

In the beginning...

Let's back up for a moment and address those of you who are in the infancy stage of your business planning. You are just formulating your ideas, and there is a whole lot running around in your head. The first question many ask is, "Where do I go for help?" and there are several good answers.

If you have set aside some funds during this process, be sure to consult financial professionals to help you get started. They will advise you on the details of a business plan and the extent to which they can help in the writing process. Often they will recommend other professionals who might be of assistance. They may even be able to discuss the viability of the business itself. Professionals they will refer you to may include attorneys familiar with business start-ups and patent attorneys, if applicable. Whatever your situation, ask for specific recommendations. Those who have been in business for many years bring the added benefit of knowing many other professionals through their networking, a topic I discuss below.

When funds are tight, there are good agencies — some state-funded — that can offer general assistance. SCORE, for example, provides teams of business advisors who can answer some of the very same questions cited above and who will often get involved in the loan process should your business require additional capital. Most of their services are free of charge. Locate an office near you at www.score.org/ and look for their occasional free seminars led by outside third parties on various business topics.

Don't forget to ask other business owners you know about how they proceeded on the path to becoming entrepreneurs. There may be gems of information here and at the very least, good contacts to the professionals they used in establishing their businesses.

Once you have opened the doors to business, there can be no greater or less expensive way to advertise than by joining a professional networking group. Whatever the format, these groups offer you a forum where you can advertise your business in front of a large audience and interest others in your service or product. In the best groups, it's as if you have engaged a light sales team for very little cost.

The mix of professionals in some groups brings greater results than others. Often, only time will tell. Give yourself a reasonable time frame — a minimum of six months — from when you join to when you expect to see some leads come your way. If after that time you have not been led to new business, move on and find yourself another group. There are many.

The trade-off in joining small groups vs. large groups is this: there is power in numbers. While joining an established large group has the advantage, you may be up against some competition or not even be able to enter at all because of the group's non-competitive rules. (i.e., only one person per given profession can become a member. If your profession is already represented, you need to look elsewhere). A small group requires more effort and leadership as you all work to increase the number of professional members. Ultimately, it may take only one or two people in the group to make the extra effort worthwhile. Such people are often referred to as "power part-

ners." They are professionals who are a perfect fit to
your business. For example, the arbitrator who dis-
covers a matrimonial attorney is a great power partner because of the people he or she comes in contact
with. Or perhaps it's the interior designer who partners with a real estate agent servicing a wealthy
book of clients. Bottom line — look for a professional
networking group in your area.

Last, but not least, there is engaging a business
coach. A coach can be a valuable asset whether at the
start-up phase or later in the business cycle. Here
you will want to research carefully as a hefty price
tag is often involved. When you find someone who
clicks with you, however, you gain a worthwhile
sounding board, not to mention an ally who can provide years of business know-how to guide you down
the right path. Notice that I mention "years of business." Can you find a 30-years-old to give you great
advice? I'm sure you can but the odds are probably
in your favor if the coach is older and has acquired
more business and life experience. My time spent
with a business coach has been invaluable. Again,
ask other professionals — whether personal connec-

tions or fellow networking group attendees. They're sure to lead you to some great resources.

When you put all of these resources together, you are on a great path to developing a sound business plan. And remember, if at first the results are not to your liking — re-think the plan, come up with new strategies, cut costs where possible, pursue revenue streams you may not have thought possible, renegotiate contracts, seek out new professional contacts but most of all —

Keep the dream alive! You can do it.

III ACCEPTABLE AND UNACCEPTABLE RISK

One of my favorite movie characters appears in *And Justice For All*. In the 1979 film, actor Jack Warden portrays a judge with a distinct peculiarity. Taking risks is one of his greatest pleasures. For instance, he enjoys eating his lunch perched on the windowsill of his office, several stories high. The most dramatic example of his love of risk-taking occurs when he shows off his piloting skills to a colleague, played by Al Pacino. Up in his Cessna, Warner turns to Pacino and says, "You see, I calculate how many miles the fuel will take me, divide it in half, and then go one mile further. Then, I head back. The real fun occurs when I see whether I can actually make it back safely." The look on Al Pacino's face is priceless as he realizes that he may be facing his own death.

Needless to say, the two make it back but not before surviving a semi-crash landing that leaves them relatively unharmed. And since these scenes are played for laughs by fine actors, the audience is hugely amused.

And now back to business. Chances are you are not launching your business venture as a sole proprietor. You may have partners as well as employees. Like the judge in *And Justice For All* you are not traveling alone. Evaluate your risks carefully. You cannot take your innocent employees and possibly uninformed partners on a ride that places them in peril.

The judge in the film felt entitled to take all of the risks he wanted. So where did he go wrong? He didn't inform his colleague of his fuel strategy before the plane left the ground. Al Pacino went along on a dangerous ride, without being an informed participant.

You too will undoubtedly take risks. Your partner(s) may well go along for the ride. But the risks need to be out in the open and decisions made together. You and your partners may play different roles in the company, but communication is essential. Establish a communicative relationship from day one. Set up weekly meetings in which to share ideas and catch up on the latest information. Arrange regular dinner meetings, where you can share your thoughts in a neutral environment. You won't regret it.

And, if you've never seen the film, do so, and watch masterful actors turn risk-taking into an art form.

IV THE IMPORTANCE
OF DAY-ONE MONEY

L et's take a step back and look again at your plan. If it shows a positive cash flow, it's for the following reasons: either you have projected a healthy amount of revenue in excess of expenses or you are well capitalized, or perhaps both.

What does it mean to be "well capitalized"? My client Veronica, who owns a pastry shop in New York City, can tell you. When we first met she was entering the planning stage. From the start Veronica was in a somewhat unusual and wonderful position: she had more than enough money to start the business.

She was prepared to start the business with $50,000 of her own money and, along with her healthy sales projection, she would have a moderate but positive cash flow. In looking over her plan for the year, I noted that while she did show a modestly positive cash position over many months, she also projected a few months that were quite tight and dipped into the red.

She mentioned that although she could put in more of her own money to start, she didn't feel it was necessary. In examining her plan further, I realized that it was time for a chat.

"Veronica, it appears that you haven't budgeted for several things. First, I don't see the cost of a part-time bookkeeper. Second, you have budgeted for a store manager at 6 hours per day when the store is open for 12 hours. Haven't you missed something?"

"No," she replied. "Nothing is missing. To save money, I am going to try to do my own bookkeeping and I will work as the store's manager for the second shift."

"I see," I replied. "When you and I first spoke, you were very excited about your role as entrepreneur and in particular, your time spent marketing the business. Do you remember that?"

She had but she hadn't yet made the connection.

"Veronica, have you determined how much money you save by not hiring a bookkeeper?"

"Yes," she said, as if she were about to reveal a number in the millions of dollars. "About $10,000 per year. Isn't that incredible?"

"Amazing," I answered in my most sarcastic tone. "Now I want you to figure out what you save by not hiring a second manager. Then add it all up. When you have, let me know how much time you will have taken away from marketing your business." I also asked her to imagine, based upon her marketing plan, to estimate how much in new business she may not have earned as a result of her "cost-saving" measures.

Needless to say, once she put these facts and figures down on paper, she could see that she would be behind the eight ball if she made the cuts she had originally planned.

I like the term "Day-One Money." It says: remember that the extra cash you set aside so you can work *on* your business — not *in* your business (as Michael Gerber would say (*Ibid*) — can make the difference between staying in business and watching it slip away.

So if your own great business plan is telling you that you may be undercapitalized, i.e., that you lack sufficient cash to start the business, what do you do? As I said earlier, you re-work the plan, perhaps over and over again. It may mean that you need to find new sources of funds. Either way, you're going to do what is necessary to keep your dream alive, and to keep it alive you will carve out a practical and well-thought-out plan.

V SPEND LITTLE, INVEST A LOT

Remember the expression: "Invest your money wisely"? Or maybe you are more familiar with: "Spend your money wisely"? After all, one of the reasons I'm writing this book and giving you these tips is that I want you to spend your money wisely from day one!

What are some of the ways to invest your money or shall I say spend your money wisely? Let's begin by considering marketing. All too often I have seen clients spend too little on marketing their business and think too little about the value of marketing. Some years ago a new client, Larry, asked me to look over his books and records, get a general overview, and identify where any problems might lie. A few hours later, I walked into his office, his American Express bills in hand.

"I know what you're going to say, Ken. These bills are too high and on occasion I have charged items that appear to be borderline personal expenses as opposed to business-related expenses."

"Larry," I said," the problem I see is not that these credit card bills are too high but that they are too low."

Judging from the look on his face, I could have been from another planet.

"Too low," he said. "How can that be?"

Knowing that he had never hired a marketing or public relations firm, I asked why I wasn't seeing any business expenses for entertainment, networking, or general marketing. How do you expect to grow the business unless you're spending some amount of money on these things? Clients and potential clients need to be taken to dinner every so often. There are social events to be attended. None of this can be accomplished unless you spend some money doing so.

"You may be right," I said. "Perhaps you are spending too much and what I should have said is that you are not investing enough.

There are ways to invest and ways to spend. Hiring the right staff, seeking advice from outsiders (even when you have to pay them), engaging a professional to assist in writing your business plan, working with a coach when things don't seem to be going your way. These are investments that will pay off.

Don't hire the first contractor you find if you sense that something doesn't sound right. Someone in your childhood taught you some good sense. Use it. Intuition? You bet! In addition to schooling and the knowledge we acquire during our years on Earth, intuition plays a major role in our decision-making. If you sense that advice is rotten, trust your instincts and move on. If you later discover that you were mistaken in thinking that the initial advice you received was wrong, so what? We all make mistakes. But I would be willing to bet that most of the time you were right. What are we really talking about is minimizing risk? Trusting your intuition will help you to do that.

Treat every decision as a major decision but not an irreversible one. If you always remember that you're investing your money — not just spending it — good decision-making will be in your back pocket.

As mentioned in Chapter IV, business-plan writing is an investment. In the December 2008 issue of *Entrepreneur Magazine*, Bart Hendricks wrote an article entitled, "Do you really need a business plan? " He talked to many business owners and to people who were planning new ventures. He quotes one business owner who says, "I was very skeptical about the value of business plans. But after looking at data compiled in various studies, [I noted that] a survey of more than 800 people all in the process of starting businesses found that writing a plan greatly increased the chances that a person would actually go into business."

And in the current difficult economic times, getting your business plan on paper, and writing it properly, is even more essential. New issues come into play, which do not arise in better times. The credit market is tighter than ever. If you're business plan calls for major outside funding, you may need to reconsider your plan during a difficult economy.

This poses some real challenges for the new business owner. Simple questions such as, "Do I have what it takes financially to get into business?" come into play. Finding new sources of investing as well as digging deeper into your own pocket to make the plan work all may factor into the equation. You can always find a handful of experts in print or the media, who downplay the concept of business plan writing. But I can assure you that in nine out of ten articles writers promote the use of a business plan very highly.

So go forth and invest. In fact, you have already made an investment by reading this book. At this very moment, you have invested a lot and spent little.

VI BRING ON THE ACCOUNTANTS

As the owner of an accounting service business, I hold the dos and don'ts of hiring accountants close to my heart. I'm particularly interested in internal accounting. To help you gain an understanding of the process, let's look at the hiring of bookkeepers and controllers.

First estimate the amount of time needed for someone to attend to bookkeeping. Take an educated guess. When you're ready to call on someone, ask the candidates for the job for their estimate of the hours required. Then you will have a good idea who may be "low-balling" and who may be too costly.

Lots of people call themselves bookkeepers. There is the college student who for only a few dollars per hour will gladly do the recordkeeping but is probably still learning on the job. At the other end of the spectrum is the highly experienced bookkeeper that comes at a higher price.

Let me describe whom I hire at my firm and why. Any bookkeeper I send to a client must have at least ten years of experience. In addition, he or she must be proficient in several different accounting software programs — including the latest versions. Most importantly, I hire "hand-holders" — people who understand that many entrepreneurs are in the dark about finance and accounting. They understand that to make clients feel comfortable, they cannot hover over the computer as if their work was a big secret. Instead, they know to invite the business owner to look over their shoulder so that they can learn what their accountant is doing. It's all about providing a comfort factor to the owner.

There is another reason why it's important to hire experience and why it serves my model so well. I view an experienced bookkeeper as a "budding" controller whose expertise has earned this title. It is reassuring for business owners to know that their bookkeeper is not only a data entry expert but is also capable of offering meaningful suggestions and comments.

Look for these same qualities when hiring account-ants. Remember, knowledge is power and you always want to make good investments with your money. Using the services of knowledgeable professionals brings power to your company. The information they impart can help you make other smart business decisions. This is another example of investing your money, not just spending it.

Let's take a look at a higher level of accounting service, that of the controller. When I started my business I offered an unusual model to small businesses: the part-time services of a controller. Many business owners believe that until they can afford a full-time controller at an annual salary of about $100,000 (plus benefits), they will need to struggle along without one. When I describe my business, I see listeners' eyes light up. "Oh, that's really unusual," they say. What they mean is, "I never realized that this sort of service existed."

Why use a controller from Day One even though you probably won't need a full time person at first? A part-time controller can ensure that you're making sound business decisions and can be a business monitor, who provides services on a quarterly basis. As time goes on and your business grows, your need for a controller may grow as well. As you continue to expand you will have to decide whether you need to engage a full-time controller or whether you need to add more hours to the part-time person's schedule. Consider paying for what you need and not more.

I would be remiss if I didn't mention business plans yet one more time. Long before your business becomes an ongoing entity, use a higher-level accounting professional to assist with the writing and updating of your business plan. There is no better time to pay for such services than at this early stage. We have already talked about the essentials of business plan writing in earlier chapters. It may be a good idea to re-read them with an eye toward understanding the importance of a business professional in your life at this very moment.

In our discussion of hiring accountants, I have saved the best for last. When interviewing candidates, be sure to get a sense of their honesty and integrity by asking pertinent questions during the interview and check their references. Why?

You expect that anyone whose services you use in any capacity, or whose products you buy, will act in an honest manner. But why is it so important when hiring internal accountants? Unlike other professionals, accountants know the details of your finances: how much money there is in your bank accounts; what your profitability (or God forbid, the lack of it) is; and perhaps even the passwords to your bank accounts. The agent who sells you insurance should be an honest person who acts with integrity but he or she will not be privy to your personal finances. Accountants will. Interview with this in mind.

If you are blessed with a keen sense of financial matters, hiring an accountant should be a relatively simple process because you have the ability to think on a similar level. However, if you — like Betsy from Chapter II — are not, follow these simple guidelines and you will be on your way to hiring the right professional.

VII THE CONVERTIBLE
OR "TOP-DOWN" THEORY

As the manager of your own business, you are in control — or you should be. So then why is this key statement so widely misunderstood? "Everything that happens in your company — good and bad — is a result of something you did or failed to do."

When this came up in a conversation with my client Eric he gave me that old "two-headed" stare.

"How is that possible?" he asked. "There are several things that don't work well within my company and most of them are due to a lack of performance on the part of my employees."

When I asked for an example, Eric told me the following:

"Well, take my bookkeeper, for one. She's very sweet and I like her but she probably only does about 75 percent of the total job. I don't think that she is skilled enough on the computer and it holds her back. I asked her to reorganize her office on several occasions and she has yet to do it. So if she were more knowledgeable and efficient, I would get faster and more accurate reports. She's been here for over a year and I think I can assume that things won't change. So you see, its not that I'm not doing my part, but there are certain things that I really cannot expect from her at this point."

If you are shaking your head in disbelief — good, you're one of the lucky ones. I cannot count the number of people who don't get it and wind up in the same situation as Eric.

"Wow," I said to him. "Let me explain why you need to start hiring right." First I asked the procedural questions (those Human Resource questions about proper written warnings and documentation). Then I told him that there was a simple reason why the accounting was not going well. "You haven't fired her yet!"

"Yeah, I know," Eric said, "but she's really nice and I just hate to fire people."

It did not take many visits to realize that this same problem affected several departments. Because Eric just hated to terminate people he kept things going at the same inefficient pace. He even held on to an under-performing family member. OUCH! A later chapter will explain the exclamation.

"Do you see, Eric, that the problem here is not your employees' but your own?"

I passed on a little business proverb I heard many years ago. "You can either learn to fire people when it's necessary or get yourself a business partner who will."

This is your business, and sometimes you need to make tough decisions. Decide whether you are cut out for it. Know yourself. Perhaps you are like Eric and need to bring someone into the company who will do what you can't. More on this subject later.

The bottom line — someone has to do the dirty work so decide who it will be.

As you read on you will see many examples of the dos and don'ts of good business practice. If you are an established entrepreneur, and some of the don'ts sound all too familiar, ask yourself why that is so.

When describing the problems your business is facing, don't start the sentence with, "If only he could do...." If you have ever said things like, "I've told them countless times and still they don't do it right." Stop yourself immediately. Begin the sentence with "I" and end the sentence with words that assume responsibility. But don't despair. By the time you've finished this book, you will be ready to fix the problems.

On a more upbeat note, I recommend rewarding yourself for all of the good decisions you've also made. Rewards come in all sizes; from the donut that you told yourself you shouldn't eat to a vacation in the Bahamas. Why wait for someone else to complement you? Do it yourself.

And so, to recap: Everything that happens in your company — both the good and the bad — is your responsibility. Own up to the problems. They are indeed your own. This attitude marks the start of healthy thinking and good decision-making.

Let's make a clear distinction between "responsibility" and "blame". You are ultimately the responsible person. If you did everything in your power to avert a bad situation but still made a mistake, it's not a question of "blame". Introduce blame and you're less likely to see the picture clearly and less likely to address the problem squarely. What is called for is to carefully evaluate where problems occur and then to take action to fix them.

Blame is rarely useful in business; there is simply no room for a term that sets off negative emotion. Positive thinking rules every day.

And when times are good, recognize that things are going well and pat yourself on the back for the good management decisions that you have made — and read on.

VIII   OH, BROTHER!

$\mathbf{T}$his chapter could just as well be titled, "Oh Sister!", "Oh Uncle!", or some other relation. But when I think of the subject I'm about to discuss, what most comes to mind is, "Oh, no!"

Yes, it's the old subject of family matters. This chapter is a good one to keep in mind no matter whether you are in the infancy stage or the mature stage of developing your business. Hiring family can bring rewards or dangers, if not planned properly.

Ladies and gentlemen, boys and girls, there is no doubt that some families work happily together in business. Often these are partnerships that were developed as family businesses from day one: the husband and wife who dreamed of opening a business together, the loving brother and sister who started an exciting venture — there are a myriad of examples. Family businesses can be as successful as any other but they present the added challenge of separating your personal life from your working life.

Someone I know has a successful career in counseling family businesses. Acting as part financial expert, part psychologist, she advises clients on everything from starting up to dispute resolution. She always has plenty of booked business because of the many controversies that can arise among families working together; they seek her services because they did not plan properly.

Then there's the case of the owner of a long-standing business who never intended to hire family until a situation arose. One scenario involves an out-of-work family member. Feeling some familial obligation, the owner put him to work. In other cases, owners brought a family member into the business without outlining a clear division of work responsibilities from the start. The results: unhappy employees and an unhappy owner. It is a mistake to assume that a family business needs less planning and division of responsibilities than a non-family business.

One family business owner I worked with credited the success of the business to the segregation of duties that he created on Day One. "Yes, we are family," he said, "but this is a business, and we figured out a long time ago that unless we treated it as such, our family would be worse off."

A client of mine illustrates another familiar scenario: the son or daughter who is being groomed to assume the business in years to come. Jamal is an example. When I first met with him, my impression was that he was a smart, sophisticated, and likeable guy. His father's company, which manufactured electrical parts, had been around for more than fifteen years serving mainly the West coast of the United States. Now they were about to open an office in New Jersey to service the East Coast.

As we talked I began to wonder if Jamal was out of his element. Here was this bright guy who was being put in charge of establishing a new office and manufacturing plant from soup to nuts. So what was his experience?

Jamal had only been working in his father's business for the past eighteen months. Prior to joining the family business he had held a supervisory position in an entirely different industry — a graphic design firm. A light bulb went on in my brain. No wonder he seemed to be making some poor decisions. It wasn't his fault. His father thought that eighteen months of business background (and a completely different business, to boot) provided enough experience to run an entirely new division of the company. Kudos to Jamal's father that he thought so highly of his son. As a practical decision, however, it was a little hasty and put the business in the hands of a somewhat inexperienced person. No doubt there are those who are able to learn a trade by being thrown to the wolves but few people have the ability to run an entire business using this method. Apparently Jamal's father's decision to keep it all in the family came before a sound evaluation of the person assuming the role.

Over the years Jamal used my financial services as a controller but more than that, he relied upon my guidance on a business management level. And so kudos to Jamal for realizing that he needed a more experienced hand to help him make certain decisions.

Family business stories can indeed end on a happy note.

IX MONEY MATTERS

Suppose you've been in business now for some time. You've been following your business plan, and operations seem to be running smoothly. Then a few bumps in the road arise. How are you as a business owner going to meet the challenges? What decisions are necessary and what new policies and procedures need to be implemented? Let's consider a few possible scenarios, specifically those that center on the issue of money. At the heart is the control of your money, how fast it comes in the door — and how fast it goes out, getting paid by your customers, and in particular, any collection problems that may ensue.

First, let's talk about incoming cash and collection. There can be many reasons why your customers have not paid your invoices. Let's assume for the moment that they have nothing to do with the quality of product or service you provide. Other factors, including a poor economy and economic conditions specific to your client's industry can certainly contribute. Or perhaps clients are financing their own cash-flow crunches via their vendors. If you happen to be one of their vendors, it's your invoice that may get shifted to the bottom of the pile.

Many business owners make a simple mistake: they continue to do business with customers who are significantly behind in payments. Granted, there may be special circumstances that call for continuing to do business as usual, but in most cases, production (whether service-time or manufactured widgets) must come to a temporary halt! I say "temporary" because the hope is that payment can be collected and business can resume.

As the owner of a business that provides internal accounting services, I assign my staff to the offices of various clients. When a client goes too long without paying my invoices I begin with a gentle reminder. After the stage of friendly reminders has passed I inform the delinquent clients that I cannot continue to send my employees to their office. If necessary, I inform them that beginning on a specific date our work for them will stop until all open invoices are paid. I emphasize that this is not a personal issue but a business decision, and that our hope is we can get back to working for them soon.

Some business people I respect feel that they must walk on eggshells around their customers. They fear that confronting customers will only alienate them. As one client put it, "This is a very good customer and I need the business."

Let's think about that statement. How good a customer is this? Perhaps he or she is a name in the industry and could recommend other clients. Imagine if every one of your customers fit that description! You would be using your valuable resources to satisfy them while your business tanked! And what about those potential referrals? Marketing experts often say that clients usually refer those that most resemble themselves in their business dealings. In his popular business books, Brad Sugars rates customers on an A, B, or C scale (*Instant Referrals*, 2006). He recommends getting rid of the C-level customers because they tend to breed more C-level customers. If this is the case, my client needs to correct his criteria for determining a good customer. By the way, paying bills late is not the only characteristic of

C-level clients. They may lack other important characteristics of A-level and even B-level customers. The bottom line: you may have clients that possess many wonderful attributes but at the end of the day, if you don't get paid, you have no business.

In contrast, let's consider another client, David, the owner of a digital marketing firm. Once he had reviewed his list of unpaid invoices and realized just how far past due some of them were he called on me to contact the late-paying customers. He asked me to inform them that if he did not receive a check for payment in full within one week, he would cease all work until the account was put in good standing. By the way, the customer was a huge multinational company while David's was a small-scale firm. Nonetheless, David knew that he needed to confront this issue head on.

Let's turn our focus to outgoing cash and expenses. Successful businesses know how to control them. Rather than delve into every type of expense a business can incur, let me outline some basic rules. First, let's distinguish between fixed and variable expenses. Fixed expenses are those that do not change no matter how much revenue you bring in. Rent is one example. Your landlord doesn't care whether or not you've made your sales quota this month. And if you triple your sales any given month, you pay the same rent. Payment is determined by the terms of your lease. Variable expenses are those that fluctuate under certain conditions. If your business entails frequent travel to your customers, your travel expenses will fluctuate based on the number of customers you have. The most common example of variable expenses is the commission companies pay to their salespeople. Such commissions are paid only when sales are generated.

What do you need to know about these two pools of expenses? First, what is the total amount of your fixed expenses? This amount is known as a company's breakeven. This fixed expense total reveals the total sales dollars necessary to make a "zero" profit. In other words, assume for a minute that you have no variable expenses. Your fixed expenses exist with or without sales, and you know that you must bring in a certain amount in revenue in order to cover these expenses.

This information alone conveys the greater importance of fixed costs over variable ones. Fixed costs
must be kept under control, and a good plan needs to
exist from day one so that you can cover your fixed
costs multiple times over. As for variable costs, let's
take a closer look. Surely you want to travel with a
budget in mind or come up with a commission com-
pensation plan that is fair but not too aggressive. Variable costs wouldn't exist without the sales to cover
them. Put another way: high variable costs indicate
high revenue, therefore, a lesser concern.

Whether you are a start-up business or an established one, controlling fixed expenses is essential.
Imagine a business that is growing year after year.
What a great feeling it would be to know that your
rent is fixed for ten years. You're sitting pretty knowing that next year you won't need to pay your landlord one penny more in rent than you do now.

The subject of cash control and expenses would not
be complete without a discussion of the remedies
available when cash is in short supply. Earlier in the
chapter I referred to customer receivables. Suppose
you are in a credit market that has slowed down

your collections. Although no one customer is taking advantage of you, the money is simply not coming in the door at the same pace as before. If your customers are paying slowly, no doubt you will be paying your own vendors slowly as well. What remedies are available?

Let's start with the best one, known as financing through your vendors. The procedure is simple: call your vendors. Tell them conditions are tight, that you have every intention of paying them 100 percent, but you'd like another 30 days to pay the bill. This step can secure 30 days of credit for free. Will all your vendors cooperate? Probably not, but some will. Why not give it a try? You're not in any worse shape if they turn you down.

Short of financing through your vendors, you can turn to the credit market and to borrowing. No one likes to do this but taking this route is often inevitable. You might arrange an overdraft line attached to your checking account. If you predict that your need for financing will be very short term, you might consider making a personal loan to the company through a low-cost (or even interest-free) credit card. Whether or not this approach makes sense from a tax standpoint depends on the how your company is legally structured. Consult your tax accountant for the best advice.

If you're digesting this information about collections and payments, you are probably thinking that there is a contradiction here. You would be correct. "If I'm staying on top of my customers about collections, won't they be doing the same to me when it comes to the bills that I have to pay?"

The answer is a definite "maybe." You might be able to have it both ways if you're lucky enough to find vendors with deep pockets who will agree to finance your bills. No doubt it takes some juggling. What is needed is to keep your eyes and ears open for any means of obtaining low-cost financing. At the same time you will try to limit the amount of time you extend to your own customers for deferred payments.

The bottom line is to strive to achieve a greater cash intake than cash outflow. It sounds simple but not always achievable. Consider those businesses whose revenue is cyclical or seasonal. For them, no more important tool exists than the cash flow projections I talked about in Chapter II. Your revenue may be seasonal but your vendors are going to expect payment nonetheless. Your projections will highlight exactly when you are going to need outside financing in order to get by in the lean months. While it may be the norm for some companies to exist on a permanent basis with seasonal or fluctuating income, it is still essential to understand the timing of incoming and outgoing money.

X   IN TIMES OF TROUBLE

I t is easy to go astray during a serious economic downturn. Business owners question their day-to-day decisions when faced with poor economic conditions. The lesson to be learned at this time brings us right back to the importance of a formal business plan.

From what I see and read, it appears that too many business owners sit back and wait to see how the economy will affect their business. This is the wrong approach to take. During hard times follow your business plan as closely as possible. There is a saying going around that applies to a troubled economy: "I hear that there is a recession going on . . . but I am not participating." I second that opinion and I, for one, live by it every day.

More people need to understand the concept of two steps backward and three steps forward. As I've said before, you need both a business and a marketing plan. The goal of your marketing plan is to increase revenue and move your business three steps forward. While a poor economy may take its toll on your business and send it two steps backward, imagine where you would be if you failed to follow your business and marketing plans. You would wind up taking the two steps backward and making no forward progress at all. Wouldn't you prefer a net gain of one step forward?

It's no good sitting behind a desk and wondering to what affect the economy will have on your business. Business owners need to understand the importance of being proactive. Don't get me wrong. This does not mean ignoring what a failing economy can do to your business but the focus must be on looking for ways to mitigate the effects.

So what steps can you take when the economy bears down on your business? First, it's a good time to review your original business plan. Your mission and your goals may remain the same whether the economy is strong or weak. What may change is how you approach achieving those goals. Take a look at your marketing plan. Your business may look the same but have your competitors' changed? Perhaps you discover that some competitors are no longer in business and you need to find ways to pick up their market share. Others may have taken on new products and are encroaching on your territory. Are the competition's products better than or inferior to your own? Dispatch a team of secret shoppers to find out. What if they report that the competitors have the advantage? Wouldn't you prefer to know the truth so that you can plan a response? Perhaps it's a matter of becoming a better marketer. I may not be a marketing expert but I do know that you may need to consult one who can point you in the right direction.

Take the experience of my client Tyler who manufactures bath and soap products. At a meeting with a prospective client, he told me, he gave a pitch for a new product, one that was not entirely new to the industry. He wanted my feedback on why I thought he had failed to convince this company to order his product. Tyler and his business partner compared notes about the potential client's personality and where they might have gone wrong in presenting their product. They concluded that the company had selected another bid because it thought the merchandise was superior. Tyler was scratching his head because he and his partner were convinced that the competitor's product was inferior to their own.

I offered the following observation. "Tyler, I was not present for your proposal so I can only guess what went on in the potential clients' heads. What I suspect is that you need to consider something more important than gaining insight into their personalities. Apparently your competition has done a better job of marketing its product. (Recall the pizza owner with the best pizza on the block). I don't know what makes its product better — if anything — but it looks like the manufacturer has done a darn good job of convincing everyone that it is. My advice to you is to focus less on your pitch and more on your competitor's advantage."

Knowing your competition is important in any economic environment. When the economy is in the dumps, however, you're looking to boost your business. This is precisely why it's so important to review your business and marketing plans with an eye to the competition. Tyler concluded that he had not done enough homework prior to his presentation.

Doing more homework is exactly what is needed in times of trouble.

Marketing is just the tip of the iceberg in a product-related business like my friend Tyler's. Some other steps to consider taking include renegotiating your lease with your landlord, negotiating for better pricing with parts or supplies vendors, and reconsidering your own pricing structure for products. A savvy accountant friend of mine, for example, devotes much of her business to helping clients determine — product by product — where their greatest profitability lies.

One of my favorite reruns of *I Love Lucy* is the episode in which she and her best friend Ethel go into the salad dressing business, bottling their own concoctions and then delivering them door-to-door on roller skates. Their dream crashes when their husbands get involved and do what Lucy and Ethel had never thought of doing. They calculated their profitability — or lack thereof — and found that the duo was actually losing money with every bottle sold. What seems hilarious on television does not look so funny in real life when you happen to be the business owner.

As for you lucky entrepreneurs in the service busi-ness arena, you too need to evaluate your fixed costs such as rent and to consider the possibility of rene-gotiation. While those in a service business don't have parts and products to cost evaluate, they do need to pay particular attention in the not-so-good times to the cost of employees and contractors who are an essential part of the services offered. Is their pay scale realistic in the present-day market? No one likes a pay cut but when times are tough, it may be necessary to ask employees to make some adjust-ments, too. It's not easy to broach this subject, even if you consider yourself a tough businessperson, and it may go against everything you believe in to cut a loyal employee's paycheck. Consider approaching them this way: have an honest conversation and treat them as partners in your business. Apologize if nec-essary and assure them that when conditions turn around, you plan to improve pay. Emphasize that you need team players right now. You might be pleas-antly surprised by the positive responses you get.

What about negotiating with your contractors in order to get the cost down and put more in your pocket? Sometimes you can. The economy has hit my own business in a few distinct ways. I have come across some prospective clients looking for a bargain. There are some who believe that in this market they may not need to pay the full asking price for our services. Some may have a number in mind that falls far from the mark. Others propose a more reasonable discount. As a business owner, I need to evaluate just how far I can go. On at least one occasion I have gone to one of my subcontracted bookkeepers to ask whether they would be willing to chip in a few dollars and reduce their fee so that we can get a new client in the door. Subcontractors differ from employees. They essentially control their hours and their prices. I have never begrudged a contractor who turned me down. Everyone's life situation is unique, and it's not for me to judge someone's decision. But as a businessman, I see it as my duty to at least make the effort.

Whether you are selling salad dressing or accounting services, revisit each aspect of your plan. When the original strategy shows some fault lines because of the economy, make adjustments. Consult a marketing expert, a business coach, or other professional. Downturns in the economy can play some funny games with your outlook and attitude so you need to seek out fresh eyes. Start each day by saying, "Here is what I'm going to do about my business today!" In other words, decide to do what it takes to get back into the groove of your business plan. While you may stumble, you will not let yourself fall.

Imagine what a positive attitude can do in times such as these. And like me, try to subscribe fully to the notion that there is a recession going on . . . but I am not participating.

XI WORKING ON YOUR BUSINESS: LET'S REVISIT

Let's get back to Michael Gerber's eloquent quote about working on your business as opposed to in your business (*Ibid*) Nothing is more important than to use your time wisely, whether it's through marketing, sales strategies, public relations, hiring, etc. The key is to draw the line between tasks that move the business forward and those that do not.

You need to be aware of what I call "administration pitfalls." If your role in a partnership is administrative, then spending time on nonproductive tasks is inappropriate. If you are a sole practitioner or one of several non-administrative partners, however, your first and foremost task is to work on your business. Administrative tasks do not fall into that category. If the responsibility for invoicing customers, for example, falls on you, it is your duty to ensure that a system that allows for quick and easy processing of that task is in place.

When I first met Ned and was introduced to his law practice, I saw how his invoicing practice was crippling his business. He alone drafted the client invoices, each one made up of details that went on for pages. An analysis of the time spent revealed that nearly 20 percent of his total working time went to writing up these elaborate invoices.

There is no hard and fast rule but I can tell you this: if you are spending more than five percent of your time on a task like this one, you need to install a new system immediately. Hiring an assistant is one possible solution. People like Ned often say, "There is no one who knows how to do this part of the job better than I do. It makes no sense to assign it to someone else." Not only is that premise false, it may explain just why this process takes so long.

Ned ultimately solved this problem (with much prodding on my part and hand-wringing on his) by recognizing that his clients didn't need the amount of detail he provided and would not view a less-detailed invoice as "second-rate."

It is a big challenge to help clients understand that administrative tasks like these do not constitute working on a business. Ned was convinced that sending invoices without details would look bad to his clients. As a result he feared that his clients would refer him less often, and then there would go the business.

Such reasoning sets up a destructive chain of reactions. Ned needed to learn that his clients measured his value not by the length of his invoices but by the services rendered as a fantastic attorney. His day-to-day briefings to his clients spelled that out for sure. Ned successfully met the difficult task of breaking years of bad habits. His is a real success story. Without taking on a partner or even an assistant, he increased gross income by 15 percent the following year. Why? Ned went back to working on his business and stopped working in his business.

Once you grasp the concept of working on your business, you will also understand the pitfalls of being a micromanager. We have all experienced such a person. As you become an entrepreneur don't become one of them yourself. While I recognize that a fair number of micromanagers are driven by psychological issues, I tend to believe that many more exist because they have failed to grasp the concept of working on their business.

The bottom line is this: you can't afford the time to be a micromanager. Develop adequate staff in each area of responsibility so that you can leave the day-to-day decision-making to them in their areas of expertise. If you catch yourself saying, "I'll just do it myself. It will be quicker," big trouble looms. Not only does micromanaging lead to an unsatisfying business life, it engenders dissatisfaction among those who work for you.

A recent documentary, *The September Issue*, focuses on the working day of *Vogue*'s Anna Wintour. This famed magazine editor and those like her are often referred to as "cold" and "driven." However you view them, they are classic examples of people who have figured out how to avoid becoming micromanagers. They are adept at putting together a team. You don't hear Anna Wintour saying, "Give me the camera. I can take a better picture myself." What you hear is someone who gives clear direction to her staff and expects 100 percent cooperation from them. Her job is overseeing the business, not becoming jack-of-all-trades but master of one.

The bitchy boss rattling off orders can seem amusing in films and stories like these. I see it otherwise. Consider the empires that they have created and ask how they accomplished it. Stepping on some toes? Perhaps. I can assure that there was less of that and more wisdom, insight, and vision than anything else. I wish that every micromanager could learn from leaders like Anna Wintour. What separates her from them is a keen sense of business along with an ability to see things from 10,000 foot above the fray.

XII   HIRE RIGHT!

I can't count the number of times business owners have asked me to examine their cash flow and advise them on whether their payroll needs to be cut in order to improve the bottom line. Here is what I tell them. Your rent may be too high for the current market, the cost of insurance may be rising, and general expenditures may need to be kept at bay. Payroll, however, should never be an issue.

Why? Let's start with the basics. Consider the case of my client Marc who provides online marketing services. He employs Mary in the creative area; John who is in charge of bringing in new clients; and Joe, another salesperson who reports to John.

"I have a few staff problems," Marc said. "I am afraid that Mary's skills are not up to snuff. I feel that Joe is not closing enough sales." Marc went on to say that Mary came from a different professional background and had never before worked with clients in the online industry. When I asked about Mary's direct supervisors, I discovered that Mary was given a chair and a desk and not much else!

"So who," I asked, "was in charge of educating Mary about the industry and leading her by the hand through her first few projects?"

Marc responded immediately. "Well, no one. At the time we needed to hire someone who could jump right into the projects, someone who didn't need much hand-holding."

Sounds to me like my client hired the wrong person. Or, if he liked Mary and thought that she showed good potential, he failed to recognize that she would need proper supervision in order to perform well.

As for Marc's take on Joe and his low sales, he said, "He is such a nice guy but when I ask his supervisor John why Joe is not more productive, he just scratches his head."

"Okay." I said. "Let's begin by having a conversation with John the supervisor. I would like to hear what he has to say."

As it turned out, it seems that John assigned most of the difficult leads to Joe, the ones that appeared to be a big stretch and the hardest to close. John kept most of the easy leads for himself. The result: Joe's statistics looked bad, while John's looked good.

I was beginning to believe that we had some classic management problems here. "We may indeed have a good salesperson in Joe," I told Marc, "but we won't find out until you hire personnel who think about what's good for the team, not just what's good for themselves."

In Chapter VII I talked about the need for business owners to take overall responsibility for their business. Marc's situation is a good illustration of the importance of taking ownership of any problems.

Whatever their role, employees need be doing their share to help the company achieve its goal of creating more sales. Even Marc's personal assistant should be up to speed. The time Marc spends doing her work represents time away from working on his business. A payroll should consist of a team of supportive members all working toward the same goal.

Evaluate an underperforming employee's performance. If you believe there is hope of leading him or
her down the right path, put in the time necessary.
Set a reasonable but limited period of time for
improvement to occur. Should performance not pick
up, move on! Remember, it's your business and no
one else's.

Let's turn for a moment to the subject of new hires.
First, the role you expect a candidate to play deter-
mines where to advertise. Various agencies and
online sites specialize in certain areas. Other sites
such as www.monster.com and www.craigslist.org
cover a wide range of jobs. Decide what best suits
your needs.

Recently I posted an ad online for a bookkeeper. For
a modest $25 investment, I received more than 50
responses. After reviewing the resumes, I chose to
interview 15 candidates — a high percentage of the
original 50 applicants. I credit the success of my ad to
a few simple factors: noting the technical qualifica-
tions needed, including proficiency in particular
software programs; the number of years of experience required; and beyond that, the personal char-

acteristics desired. When it comes to hiring a book-keeper, for example, I always mention that I am look-ing for a "hand-holder" and describe what that means to me. Disregarding the applicants who will answer any ad — whether or not they meet the qual-ifications — many know their own personalities and fit the job description.

Once interviews are lined up, be sure to prepare a list of questions in advance. During the interview lis-ten carefully to the answers you receive. If anything you hear raises an eyebrow (or even half of an eye-brow), pursue the issue until you are fully satisfied with the explanation.

I was looking for a part-time bookkeeper who could work at least three days a week. In her cover letter, one young applicant assured me that she could, and during the interview she repeated her willingness to work three days weekly. She then went on to ask whether there was some flexibility to work on dif-ferent days each week. At first I agreed. When she asked whether it would be possible to work two days some weeks and four days other weeks to "make up the time," I began to feel uncomfortable.

In this initial interview the applicant was already trying to strike deals on the agreement — warning signs that her personality was not a good match for the job. I moved on to another candidate.

It is important to recognize the advantage of holding out for someone who has all the required characteristics, not just some of them. The wider you advertise the position, the larger the population you reach, and the greater the possibility you will find a candidate who fits all the criteria you have set.

Such a plan of action decreases the odds of making the wrong hire. Whether you are hiring from scratch or evaluating an underperforming employee, remember, hire right and payroll should not be an issue!

XIII ATTENTION RETAILERS!

etail businesses come in all styles and shapes. They range from clothing stores to cell phone outlets, from street-level shops to second-floor businesses. With your knowledge of these and other retail enterprises, no doubt you will choose the best possible location for your business and will make all the right investment decisions. Correct? Why then am so baffled by the number of retailers who seem to make so many wrong moves when it comes to branding and the street-appeal of their store?

Consider Claire, a client who opened a high-end ladies clothing boutique in my hometown, Hoboken, New Jersey. After operating in one location for three years she had the opportunity to move to a larger and more visible location. Another fashionable boutique had previously occupied the space. Claire elected to retain the former tenant's color scheme of vivid aquamarine, inside and out. After a year in the new location she called me. Sales had taken an unusual decline, and she needed advice on how and where to spend her money wisely. Little did she know that I had been keeping an eye on her store. I was astounded that Claire had kept the aqua color scheme of the former tenant all this time. In addition, not only was the name of the store set in an obscure corner of the front window, the typeface of the stencil was difficult to read.

I sat down with Claire and before I could get very far, she jumped in, "We aren't too concerned about changing the store's color scheme or the appearance of our name on the window. Our core client base knows us well and knows where to find us. As for passers-by, it's our clothing and our style that attract attention."

Apparently Claire did not have a good understanding about product branding and marketing. I passed on some of the comments I had overheard in the area. One woman said that every time she passes by she assumes that the former store is still there because the color is the same. Another said that she often passes by after hours to look at the clothes in the window but she always describes the store to friends as the "aqua store" because she can't recall the new name.

Claire and I talked about branding and the need to make the store her own. Before finding out the rest of Claire's story, let's consider the experience of Jill in selling high-end paintings.

Jill opened her art gallery in the summer of 2006 and hired me as finance manager before the doors opened. She did some extensive remodeling of the space and invited me to see it a few days before the grand opening. I was shocked at what I saw even before I had opened the door from the street. The windows were a dark smoky-colored glass, and no name was visible. At first I thought that the window stencil with the gallery's name had not arrived yet. Not so.

 "We really don't want the name outside," Jill said. "We think we project a more exclusive and high-end aesthetic this way. We have a contact list of wealthy individual art buyers and we are going to rely on it to attract major customers."

Jill's attitude is an all too common example of the blind-sided approach some retailers take. Wouldn't Jill's wealthy customers patronize a gallery that posted its name out front? After all, this was a new business. Why wouldn't a retail business owner want to market to as wide an audience as possible? Jill's "aesthetic" ran the risk of cutting off the potential sales to passers-by.

The sad news is that Jill could not rely on sales to the wealthy clients on her database and was forced to close her business. Could her story have ended differently? I believe so. As for Claire and her boutique in Hoboken, her story does have a happy ending. She hired a "branding" expert four years ago and her store is thriving. I'd even say that business is downright rosy — the color of her interior, logo, and shopping bags after the big makeover. The store's name is now prominently displayed on the front window. Once Claire used my help to identify where the problems were, she put the information to good use and righted the business.

XIV SMART CLIENTS— AND WHY I LOVE THEM

H ow can you not admire smart clients? They ask all the right questions, look for new and innovative ways to run the company, and work on their business. And of course they always follow my advice! All right, perhaps not all of the time but what is most important they, like my friend Claire, combine keen interest in their business with a desire to learn from others.

What sets the most highly regarded professionals apart is that they do all of the above but also react judiciously to situations and problems as they occur. Sometimes an immediate reaction is not called for and even can be unwarranted until further research takes place. Weigh your options, talk it over among the partners, chat with other professionals. It may take a few days or even a few weeks. While there is no exact time frame for responding to a problem, don't wait months before making changes and run of risk of getting behind the eight ball. Getting behind the eight ball can lead to disaster because right behind that eight ball may be a curve that becomes even harder to recover from. Not impossible, but more difficult!

During his 12 years in office, New York City mayor Ed Koch's trademark saying was, "How'm I doing?" Everywhere he went he asked the public, his colleagues, and advisors this same question until people associated the saying with him alone. Whether his question arose out of sincerity or political strategy is open to debate. Nevertheless, business leaders need to get in the habit of raising this same question. Isn't "How'm I doing?" what smart entrepreneurs continually ask themselves and the professionals they consult?

THREE ADMIRABLE QUALITIES

When I think of the most admirable traits my clients share in common, three top the list. I list them not to applaud them — although that may be reason enough — but to provide insight into the soul of great entrepreneurs.

1. *Perseverance.* In good times and bad, prosperous days and less fortunate, perseverance keeps things afloat. Business people with a dream march on like soldiers. No amount of adversity is going to let them fall. They may stumble at times but they will recover. Mention the possibility of failure at your own risk. They have come too far and invested too much to let it all go.

2. *A standard of high quality.* Whether as owners of a product or service business, they keep one goal in mind: to provide the best products and service possible. Have you ever been to a retail store and received the impression that the owner did not really look out for customers? You leave scratching your head, wondering how he or she stays in business. The smartest clients I know treat customers with kid gloves and respect. As for high maintenance customers, it's not a question of being a doormat but of understanding how to use people skills and, if necessary, to smile politely and move on. The same high standard extends to the product they sell. Their product is a representation of their own high standards and must reflect them.

Whether selling higher- or lower-end products, they strive to achieve the best. Bottom line: they are keenly aware that it is their behavior as much as their product that makes a lasting impression.

3. *Seeking opportunities*. Woody Allen once said that 90 percent of success depends on just showing up. That's what these clients do; they show up for every meeting, appointment, and new event intent on of finding new outlets to further business. A client of mine makes a habit of reporting on every meeting he has with other professionals, many of them outside the scope of his line of work. It became apparent that he wasn't accepting these meetings just for amusement. He sees in the ideas of others the potential to expand his business. Such clients return from these meetings and events with a giddy sense of fulfillment. Do such opportunities all pan out? Certainly not. More important, however, is that these entrepreneurs firmly believe that another great opportunity is just around the corner. And why not? What a healthy way to run your business, not to mention your life.

What do you think are your chances of success if you are a persevering individual who puts the quality of your service above all else and knows how to convey that to customers, and who looks constantly for new opportunities? Pretty darn good! If you were my client, I would give you a 90+ and enter you in my smart client "Hall of Fame."

Whether it's employment issues, client-related issues, or any one of a host of other challenges, be sure to look for advice, weigh your options, take logical steps and above all remember to ask: "How'm I doing?"

XV NO SALES, NO PROBLEM!

Throughout the book I cite problems that can get in the way of achieving your sales goals. Never do I associate the word "sales" (or "revenues") with the word "problem." Now I'm going to tell you why.

A list of my favorite stories and lessons would include the following — a lesson I learned many years ago from a respected friend and colleague. It has become the basis for a question I frequently ask during the initial stages of a client-accountant relationship.

As a Controller in private industry, I have always sought to look beyond the finances of the company. While unraveling financial problems is the backbone of my work, I also look at the other issues business owners face. I consider it my responsibility to suggest they consult other professionals (marketers, public relations, salespersons) when I feel that the business is lacking.

And so, I pose this favorite questions to new and even potential clients. "What do you feel is one of the biggest problems facing your company?" Although my statistics are unofficial, my guess is that I get the same answer at least 75 percent of the time.

"If I had to choose one," says the owner, "it would have to be sales. Yes, definitely sales. I really need more revenue."

Usually they go on to explain that costs are fairly under control but lack of sufficient revenue is the number one problem.

I have to disagree, even if I don't know the business owner or the company. Sales are never a problem, they are a goal. Fix the problems and you will achieve the goal. Sales can be thought of as an eso-teric condition that can only be achieved when the planets are aligned. How do you get them aligned? First, you analyze the problems within the company so that you can locate the person qualified to assist with the solution.

This short list can help give you the idea:

- Your salespeople are not given the right incentives and therefore — poor sales. *The problem is the incentive, not the sales.*

- You have not invested any money in marketing your product but instead rely solely on word of mouth and therefore — poor sales. *The problem is in the lack of a marketing plan, not the sales.*

- You have a staff but find yourself doing most of the work. A host of problems could exist here. Ultimately though, you are wearing too many hats and therefore — you have fewer sales than you would like. *The problem is in the structure of the organization, not the sales.*

Go back to nearly every chapter of the book and identify the topics discussed. Have you heard me say that sales can be a big problem? Nope. That's because I address the bigger issues that affect sales — not the sales themselves. The problems need to be fixed, and you need to get on them before they come crashing down on you. Because ultimately, it's all about you-know-who?

As this chapter's title says, "No sales? No problem". Perhaps another way to put it is — where there are poor sales, there are likely many issues! Remind yourself that good business people run into situations like these often. And it may very well be happening to you. But you're a practical, thoughtful entrepreneur who takes responsibility. Right? Now go and solve the problems!

XVI KNOW THYSELF

There are those — and you may know some of them or even be one of them yourself — for whom change does not come easily. Perhaps there are psychological factors at the root. There are times in my career when I have had to be part psychological counselor and part financial advisor but my purpose here is not to delve into what makes people tick. There is no diploma in psychology hanging on my walls.

For some people change comes slowly, often after much thought and painful give and take. They resist change at first but with a little arm-twisting they come to realize the problem is all too real and they plunge ahead ready to do what is best. And good for them! In Chapter XIV I mentioned that success requires not waiting too long to bring about necessary changes. Nevertheless, the "slow-changers" out there are still better off than those who resist making changes entirely.

Then there are those for whom change is impossible. They resist and resist until suddenly they find themselves in a bad situation and wonder how they're going to dig themselves out of the hole. Not only do they put their business and possibly their savings in jeopardy, but their employees as well. When I meet such resistance, I try over and over to get through. I stop urging change once I realize that it is beyond my capability as an accountant to make it happen. I find myself loving these people dearly and I have compassion for them. But all compassion in the world is not enough to bring them to make changes. I don't give up on them but try to work with them within their comfort zone.

It is these people who may view the topics in this book as good ideas but ones they can never put into practice. A new sense of self may need to come first. All kidding aside, for anyone in this category, go to the "self-help" section of your local library or bookstore. Until you start to change yourself and accept change in your life, few of the concepts in this book will come to life for you. You may recognize them as important but you will probably just nod your head, put down the book, and tell yourself that these problems belong to someone else.

In *Give it Up!* (2006) Mary Carlomagno writes about the need to give up various activities in life that are done out of habit to find the joy that abstaining can bring. While I found the book an amusing and informative read, I took away a bigger message: when you bring change to your life, windows of opportunity await you — both large and small.

A more philosophical read is Eckhard Tolle's *The Power of Now* (1999). Thousands of other books that deal with bringing change to one's life fill the shelves of bookstores everywhere. Don't be overwhelmed by the number. Try one and start reading. Once you have understood a small part of what change requires, come back to *The Practical Dreamer.*

I can imagine a reader now saying, "Are you kidding? Do you really tell clients that they need to change? Don't they resent that"? Of course, I don't say that for the simple reason that I am hired for my financial expertise, not as the company psychologist. That is not to say that if I have known someone many years and feel that they might be receptive, that I might not politely do so. For the most part, I remain silent on this subject. Writing this book has given me the freedom of mentioning the need for change without hurting anyone's feelings.

As I said at the beginning of the chapter, I never walk away from clients who are resistant to change. My job is to bring business owners good information — not to force them into decisions they are uncomfortable making. The old adage that you can lead a horse to water but you can't make him drink is certainly true. It's not my job to make clients drink but to tell them that the water is fine and they would be better off taking a sip.

If none of this sounds very familiar, then good for you. You have probably implemented or anticipate implementing some changes as you've been reading along. The practical dreamer is no doubt already living inside you.

There is another good reason for knowing oneself. When I discussed the hiring process in Chapter XII I focused on employees. Let's now turn to the subject of taking on partners. In my experience the secret to choosing a good business partner has as much to do with finding a good match for your personality as for your expertise.

You have probably heard that the approach to choosing business partners is much like choosing a life partner. Considering there is a possibility that you will spend as much if not more time at work than you do anywhere else, choose your partners carefully. To that I would add that a frank evaluation of your own personality and skills is an important guide to follow as well.

First, look for a business partner who understands and accepts your personality, not someone who is going to lock horns with you. At the same time it is important that you respect and admire them for their own qualities. People with contrasting personalities and skills can often combine their talents in ways that work to a partnership's advantage.

Long before I had my own business, I attended a seminar led by an interior designer. Although I can no longer remember the topic she discussed or why I was there, I do know that one statement has stayed with me: "To have a successful business you don't need to be a great salesperson, a great marketer, or even an expert on hiring the right people. But if you aren't, you need to get yourself a partner who is.

Otherwise, you set yourself up for failure." I like to phrase her wise advice another way. When looking for a business partner, hire your opposite. Know your own strengths and weaknesses well enough to look for someone who can provide what you cannot. The best partnerships I have witnessed are those in which members concentrate on the tasks and responsibilities best suited to their expertise and personality.

So, if you are contemplating expanding your business to include others besides you at the helm, make certain to know thyself and take the appropriate action.

XVII   THE PRACTICAL DREAMER

When it comes to personality types it is unlikely that anyone is 100 percent Type A or Type B. There lives inside of each of us the ability to be flexible, to a greater or lesser degree.

As I define it, flexibility is the ability to act outside of the box. You don't need to embrace change totally. That will come in time. All that is needed is a willingness to try a new tact. If you are reading this book because you are looking to improve your business, you already know that repeating the same thing over and over will only produce the same result. It takes a dream to begin the journey.

What is your dream? To own your own business? To double the revenue of your business within a year? Or does your practical side interrupt and say, "Wait a minute. You've got to be kidding. You can never accomplish that." Instead of letting these doubts become debilitating, hold on because there is a middle ground. Use your hesitations to temper ambitions and let them lead the way to practical decision-making. Turn those reservations around and say to yourself, "Okay, maybe my thinking was a little overblown but I can do this, even if I need to make some adjustments."

The practical dreamer says, "I can double my revenue but it may take a bit longer to accomplish this than I originally thought — and that's okay."

The practical dreamer says, "I would love to add a new and altogether different dimension to my services because it seems like fun but first I need to be sure that it's going to be profitable."

The practical dreamer says, "I want a client list of people and businesses that are changing the world but I need to be sure they are solid and can pay the bills, not bring me down."

I enthusiastically endorse aiming for the stars and making the dream of owning a business come true. With each step, remember, practicality rules the day. *Step One:* Imagine your wildest dreams. *Step Two:* Take all of the practical steps to achieving them. *Step Three:* Live the dream.

And so, here's to you — future entrepreneurs and practical dreamers I may never get to meet. If just one element, one paragraph, one small chapter of this book becomes a part of your successful model, then I have done my job. And I would love to hear from you. Let me know if your dream came true.

ADDENDUM

PUTTING IT ALL TOGETHER
A look at two businesses from 10,000 feet up

I did much of my writing at a local café in Hoboken, New Jersey, known as Ganache. Only when I was nearly done did I ask myself, "Why do I keep returning to this same spot?" Sure, I liked the food, the staff, the customers, and the general ambience. I'm a sucker for a great cup of coffee, and there was that. I enjoyed the outdoor tables located in a quiet area. Then one day a light went off. I knew that I had to include this addendum because I had suddenly understood that I have been a connoisseur of well-run businesses since I was a child.

Here I was, writing a book about learning to become a great entrepreneur. All the while I was observing operations in this café, an enterprise that seems to have made all the right moves. Perhaps my patronage had less to do with the coffee and more to do with my fascination with how the café owner conducted business. From my seat at the little aluminum table outside, I could make a case study of a retailer who seemed to personify fine entrepreneurship. Mind you, I didn't go into the kitchen nor did I talk business with the owner. From my daily perch I sat and observed.

The location: with a street entrance on the ground floor of a luxury apartment building, the café was located in a relatively quiet part of town — not so quiet, however, that it lacked good foot traffic. Within two blocks in either direction, new residential buildings are springing up with openings planned in the next six months. The café is poised to attract twice the number of customers it currently serves.

The retailer: One day, while waiting for my bagel and cream cheese, I mentioned that I'd seen a large group of construction workers all placing orders the previous day. "Oh cool!" the owner remarked. "I assigned someone else to work the register a few days ago so that I could walk over to the local construction sites. I handed out our menu to the workers and pointed out where we were located." That is to say, she took a few minutes out to work on her business instead of in her business and look at the results. I've also heard her take the opportunity to ask customers what dishes they like or don't like. The café's exterior is clearly identified in the generous awnings advertising the name. The physical changes that I've seen occur — from the way items are displayed to the choice on the menu — indicate that she is always rethinking her plan and coming up with new and better ideas. She keeps an eye open for what really works (i.e., the profitability of items) and what does not. I've also noted that she does not work in the café 24-7. She keeps her own hours and employs a staff that is capable of running things when she is not there.

The staff: Not only does the owner greet customers warmly she employs workers who are also cordial — or she has trained them well, conveying to them that the customer comes first. The staff is never idle; whether serving customers or, when the store is quiet, helping to stock the shelves, cleaning up, or taking inventory. In other words, the staff is a team that works together toward the same goal.

The economics: As a long-time observer, I can see that this business is on the rise even at a time when the economy is not in good shape. Considering the various changes I have seen take place at the café, I can't help thinking that some improvements came about after assessing the competition and adapting accordingly. A wide variety of items are for sale —

many of them offerings that are not sold at other local cafés. This suggests an owner who spends time evaluating her competition.

When I asked her how she came about opening her business, the café owner told me that she discussed her ideas first with many people; friends, family, and professionals. If this information sounds familiar, it's because it touches upon what I've recommended in nearly every chapter of this book.

Now for my second example — one that dates from my childhood. Unlike the small neighborhood café in Hoboken I just described, this is one of the world's largest and best-known enterprises.

I made my first trip to Walt Disney World in Orlando, Florida before I was a teenager. Six years later I returned with a group of friends and since then I have made three additional trips, including one last year. The word the folks at Disney like to throw around their theme park is "magic." There is the Magic Kingdom and magic shops and magical rides. When you enter an exhibit you'll often hear the commentator talk about the "magic" that Walt Disney himself set out to create.

Considering the number of times I have visited, it is clear that I like and am fascinated by Disney World. As a child I was mesmerized by everything Disney represented. I enjoyed the rides, the exhibits, the food, and of course, all those silly cartoon characters running around. As an adult, I must admit that although my love for the rides has not diminished much, now I am in awe of Disney the business. No other business of this vast scale comes to mind when I think of the perfect business. Today I like to wander about trying to come up with something the company may have forgotten to include or to discover if some aspect of the park is not quite as perfect as it could be. I can't name one. For example, the facility is kept as clean as possible. Just try throwing something on the ground and you will find a Disney employee right behind you with a broom. I was so taken with this fastidiousness that once I tried an experiment. Yes, I littered in the name of research. I threw a small piece of paper on the ground and then timed just how long it would take before someone swept it up. The answer: 44 seconds.

Their staff is about as kind and congenial as could be. Could you imagine it otherwise? Why in the world would someone work there, who didn't want to be around families and kids all day? Those hiring staff understand that the magic Walt Disney subscribed to must be shared by every employee. Only then can they make every visitor feel like the special guest that they are. By the way, the guy that swept up my trash must have noticed me because he told me with a big grin on his face, "Not to worry. I'll get that for you."

On a recent visit, I asked two employees whether they liked working for the Disney company. Both answered the same way. They smiled and said that they enjoyed being part of the Disney team. They actually used the word "team." Could their answer have been designed for the customers? Perhaps, but it seems unlikely. How could consumers feel so special if the staff didn't embrace the Disney philosophy?

Imagine what this business must have been like in its planning stages. Don't you think they had a formal business plan? Of course they did. The Walt Disney Company mission statement found on its website states that its mandate is "to be one of the world's greatest producers and providers of entertainment."

The Disney mission is a tall order and its staff works hard at making it come true.

And how about reliability? Is there anything there that does not run on a strict schedule? Whether it's the timing of the rides and the shows or when the gates open in the morning and close at night, the people behind Disney make it clear to every customer: we are reliable!

I challenge you to find any practices that I have championed in my book, which Disney World has not embraced. As for the company's scheduling and reliability, they have figured out what the public wants and they have gone to great lengths to provide it. A measure of a business's greatness is that it performs so well that it is difficult to tell whether it is a product or a service business. In Disney World's case, probably it is both.

It may be hard to find a single individual to contact at Walt Disney World if I wanted to convey my feelings of admiration but perhaps some day I will. Better yet, I will send them a copy of my book. As for my friend who owns the café, I look forward to handing her a copy personally. "Why would she buy it? I have thought to myself, "After all, I have nothing to teach her." Though perhaps she might discover a nugget somewhere that she could put to use. And it will be a signed copy that I give her. Should I inscribe it: "Thanks for being an outstanding example of entrepreneurship"? No, too big a word, and what if I misspell it. How about, "Thanks for the coffee and a nice place to sit"? Perhaps that's too simple. No, I've decided to write: "You have mastered the concept of being a practical dreamer. As your loyal customer, I thank you."

AUTHOR'S NOTE

Needless to say, there are many supportive family members, friends and colleagues to thank. But it is to my clients — past, present, and future — that I owe the most appreciation. I have known many of you through great success, while others have trod a rougher time on the entrepreneurial path. If you recognize yourself in this book, it is a testament to how much I care personally and professionally for you all. Each of you has enriched my life. Not only have I stood by you, you have stood by me. You have given me the opportunity to view your business through a magnifying glass, and I am a better person for it. Rather than mention you by name I simply say a collective "thank you."

As for others in my life that I want to name special thanks go to: Sid for standing by me during the earliest entrepreneurial years and for being a great cheerleader; David for extending his hand and his wallet when I was not able to do the same; and my family for always making me believe that I was born into the best family one can have. I thank Jim for his support as a business coach, without whom this book may never have been more than a thought; my professional team of co-workers who make me proud of the business I have created; my dogs for letting me know when I have been at the computer too long; and above all, my parents, who are no longer on this Earth but who showed me they were proud of me 24/7.

BIBLIOGRAPHY

Carlomagno, Mary. *Give It Up! My Year of Learning to Live Better with Less* (HarperCollins: New York, NY, 2006).

Gerber, Michael E. *The E-Myth: Why Most Small Businesses Don't Work and What to Do About It* (Harper Collins: New York, NY, 1995).

Horan, Jim. *The One Page Business Plan for the Creative Entrepreneur* (One Page Business Plan Company: Berkeley, CA, 2005).

Sugars, Brad. *Instant Referrals* (McGraw-Hill: New York, NY, 2006).

Tolle, Eckhard. *The Power of Now, A Guide to Spiritual Enlightenment* (Namaste Publishing: Vancouver, BC and New World Library: Novato, CA; 1999).

www.ingramcontent.com/pod-product-compliance
Lightning Source LLC
Chambersburg PA
CBHW021957170526
45157CB00003B/1029